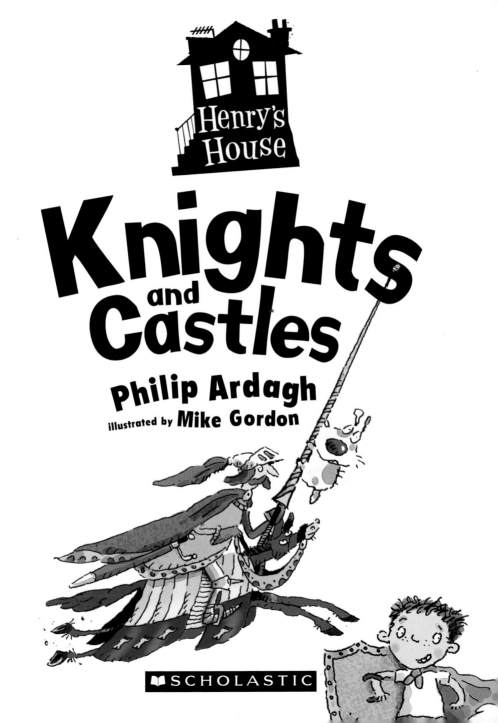

Henry's House

Knights and Castles

Philip Ardagh

illustrated by **Mike Gordon**

SCHOLASTIC

For Freddie, with fond memories of Bodiam Castle.

P.A.

Editorial Director: Lisa Edwards
Senior Editor: Jill Sawyer

Scholastic Children's Books,
Euston House, 24 Eversholt Street,
London NW1 1DB, UK
a division of Scholastic Ltd
London ~ New York ~ Toronto ~ Sydney ~ Auckland
Mexico City ~ New Delhi ~ Hong Kong

First published in the UK by Scholastic Ltd, 2010

Text copyright © Philip Ardagh, 2010
Illustrations copyright © Mike Gordon, 2010
Colour by Carl Gordon

ISBN 978 1407 10722 6

Printed and bound by Tien Wah Press Pte. Ltd, Singapore

10 9 8 7 6 5 4 3 2 1

Philip Ardagh and Mike Gordon are regular visitors to Henry's House. Philip (the one with the beard) keeps a note of everything that's going on, and even reads a mind or two. Mike (the one without the beard) sketches whatever he sees, however fantastical it may be ... and together they bring you the adventures of Henry, an ordinary boy in an extraordinary house!

Contents

Welcome to Henry's House!

To the tower!

Greetings, Jaggers! Baron Blueblood requests that you join him at once.

Baron Blueblood is the lord of this castle, Henry.

LORD AND LADY BLUEBLOOD'S ROOMS

CHAPEL

GREAT HALL

KITCHENS

DUNGEON

FOOD STORE

Blueblood Castle has changed much over the years. It started out as one big tower, called a keep.

It had very thick walls and was well guarded, to keep enemies OUT.

7

Windows and bows

Some windows were shaped like crosses.

I can fire my longbow through this long, tall slit.

And I can fire my crossbow through this crossways one.

Longbows could fire arrows much further than a crossbow could.

Crossbow arrows were called bolts. They went much faster.

BOWS NOT TO SCALE

ARROW

A crossbow bolt could pass right through you.

CROSSBOW BOLT

The Great Hall

Here we are, at the Great Hall!

But the Baron is nowhere to be seen!

It's HUGE!

What's so great about it? There's no breakfast!

The Great Hall was the biggest room in a castle.

Noblemen and noble women (lords and ladies) ate meals there.

At night, servants laid straw on the floor and slept in the hall.

11

Down in the kitchens

Spices were sometimes used to cover up the taste of meat that had "gone off".

Different foods could be cooked in a cauldron at the same time.

These people are repairing armour and weapons.

Stop that chattering, and come and help me at once!

OK, Jaggers!

15

Page duties

Are you a knight?
Don't be ridiculous! I'm Will, a squire. I look after Sir Percy. YOU must be my new page.

Er, no. But I'd like to be!
Excellent! Then you can help me sort out Sir Percy's weapons and armour.

Being a page was the first step to becoming a knight: a warrior on horseback.

1. Only boys could become pages. They were chosen from rich families.

2. A page would go to live in a castle.

3. A page would serve food in the Great Hall.

4. He would look after his squire and his squire's horse.

5. Pages and squires learnt to ride and to use the bow, sword and lance. If a page trained well, he could become a squire.

A suit of metal

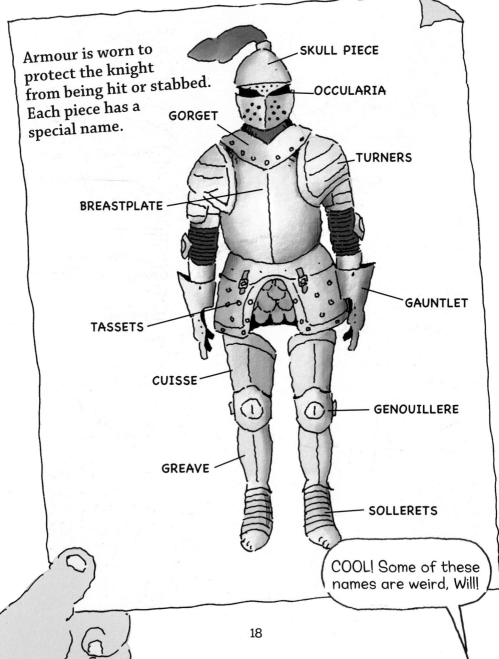

Armour is worn to protect the knight from being hit or stabbed. Each piece has a special name.

SKULL PIECE

OCCULARIA

GORGET

TURNERS

BREASTPLATE

GAUNTLET

TASSETS

CUISSE

GENOUILLERE

GREAVE

SOLLERETS

COOL! Some of these names are weird, Will!

Half an hour later...

Have you found all the armour?

I'm just missing Sir Percy's helmet, Will!

Did somebody switch the light out?

Armour got better and better over the years. The first metal armour was chainmail: hoops of metal linked together.

CHAINMAIL

Help! A robot!

Next came heavy suits of armour.

I can hardly move!

Later, armour became much lighter. The arm and leg joints were made of chainmail.

19

A broadsword was used to chop at your enemy, not to stab him. It took two hands to hold it.

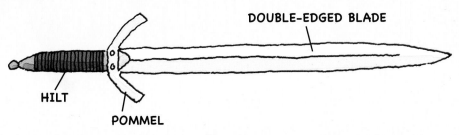

Coats-of-arms

And don't forget Sir Percy's shield. It has his coat-of-arms on it.

What's a coat-of-arms?

A jacket worn by an octopus? Or would that be a coat-of-LEGS?

Castle-owners put their own special design on the sleeveless coats that they and their knights wore over their armour. Now everyone would know who was fighting for whom.

BLUEBLOOD COAT-OF-ARMS

There are strict rules about coats-of-arms.

Each colour, pattern or shape has a special meaning.

The making and study of coats-of-arms is called heraldry.

The different bits that go together to make up a coat-of-arms have special names.

HENRY'S HOMEMADE COAT-OF-ARMS

The crest

The helmet

Another supporter

The supporter

The shield (the part of the "arms" shown on a knight's shield)

Head for Henry's House

The motto (which used to be shouted in battle!)

Who's in charge?

Chivalry

Knights were meant to live by a set of rules called chivalry.

They were supposed to be brave, generous and polite.

As well as being loyal to their lord and king, they were also supposed to look out for the poor, sick and needy.

Knights were expected to be quick to carry out "honourable deeds".

Knights were supposed to judge people by their character – what people were like – rather than how important they were.

Some knights were far better at behaving this way than others!

From squire to knight

He then spent the night praying in the chapel.

The next morning, the other squires dressed him in the finest armour.

He was then handed his spurs (which fitted on his heels).

A sword in a belt was tied around his waist.

He was now ready to be "dubbed" a knight.

Arise, Sir Hank.

The cracks in this floor could do with being fixed!

DUB!

DUB!

Within the walls

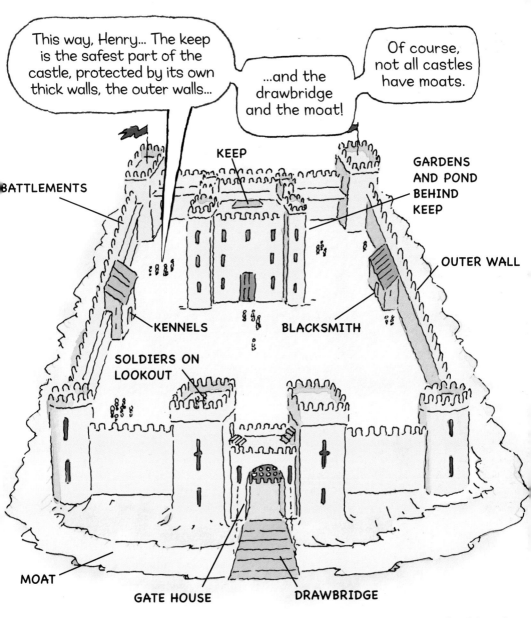

Later castles were built without keeps. All the rooms were built into the outer walls.

The round towers at Blueblood Castle were built later than the rest of the castle.

Bridging the moat

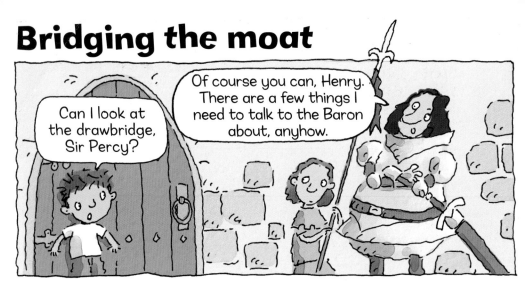

The drawbridge can be raised and lowered. When the lever is pulled to open the drawbridge, the weight goes up and the bridge comes down. The bridge is on chains.

As well as having a drawbridge, many castles had a fixed wooden bridge. It ran in line with the castle walls.

Enemy soldiers on the bridge were an easy target for the archers in the castle.

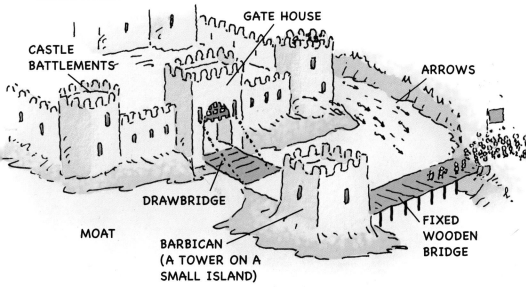

GATE HOUSE

CASTLE BATTLEMENTS

ARROWS

DRAWBRIDGE

MOAT

BARBICAN (A TOWER ON A SMALL ISLAND)

FIXED WOODEN BRIDGE

Inside and out

Do people ever swim in the moat?

You must be joking! This is where we tip all our rubbish and where waste from the garderobes goes.

A garderobe was a castle loo. It was a small room with a bench with a hole in it. All the waste fell straight into the moat.

Can I have some privacy, please!?!

Loo paper was old parchment and leaves.

The lords and ladies also used chamberpots. It was the servants' job to empty them...

... into the moat.

34

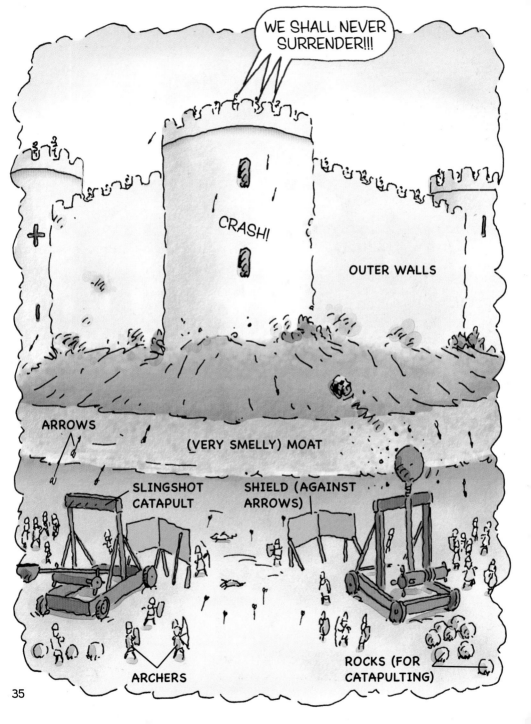

...but we WON!

VICTORY!

It's lucky Blueblood Castle has a moat, Henry. If it didn't things might have turned out very differently!

IN A CASTLE WITHOUT A MOAT

Tall ladders and siege towers could be used against the outer walls.

A siege tower could be rolled in place.

Soldiers could reach the top of the castle wall, protected from arrows.

Sometimes a tunnel was dug under a castle wall (without a moat).

WALL

TUNNEL

It was held up with pieces of wood.

When it was finished, the pieces of wood were burnt.

The tunnel collapsed and so, hopefully, did part of the wall above it.

BOOM!
No castle was safe, with or without a moat, when the bombard was invented. It was an early kind of cannon: a really big gun!

BOMBARD

Practice makes OUCH!

A little later:

All you have to do is ride at the quintain. The idea is to hit the shield with your lance, WITHOUT the sack swinging around, knocking you off!

Sounds easy enough!

THUNDERING HOOVES

I can't watch!

SHIELD (THE TARGET)

SACK (THE SWINGING WEIGHT)

QUINTAIN

ARRGHHH!

I'm f-fine. I'm OK!

THUMP!

There aren't really two of us, Henry!

A woman's world

The hunt is on!

Falconry was hunting with trained birds.

The birds were trained to catch and bring back smaller birds.

Lords and ladies hunted. They had their own birds.

HOOD

Hunting birds wore hoods until it was time to fly.

People wore a thick glove for their bird to take off and land on.

TALONS (CLAWS)

Birds often had bells fixed to their talons, so people could tell where they were.

BELLS

LEASH

44

The more important a man was, the bigger his bird.

Ladies ALWAYS hunted with a smaller bird called a MERLIN.

FOR A KING

GYRFALCON

FOR A PRINCE

FALCON

FOR A KNIGHT

SACRET

FOR A SQUIRE

LANNER

FOR A LADY

MERLIN

FOR A YOUNG NOBLEMAN

HOBBY

FOR A SERVANT

KESTREL

Hunting birds are "birds of prey" that kill other birds in the wild.

A falconer trained the birds to bring the dead bird back to their "master" or "mistress".

LEATHER LEASH

YOUNG FALCON IN TRAINING

TASTY TITBIT

FALCONER

A grown-up bird caught in the wild was called a haggard.

Huh?!

A bird trained from a chick was called an eyrie.

Mamma?

Getting ready

Jousting tournaments began as pretend battles between armies of knights. Lots of people ended up badly hurt or even dead!

Later, tournaments had more rules. There were fights on horseback, followed by a free-for-all fight on foot.

A lot of people were still badly hurt.

No tickling!

Finally, there were one-to-one jousts between knights.

Even with better rules and better armour, jousting was still VERY dangerous.

A jousting field outside a castle was called "the lists".

DRINKS TENT

SERFS STOOD OR SAT ON THE GROUND

BARON BLUEBLOOD, LORD OF THE CASTLE

TRUMPETER

GUARD

THE HERALD CALLED OUT KNIGHTS' NAMES

A lady's favour

When a knight was jousting he often wore a "lady's favour". A favour could be a coloured scarf, showing that he was fighting in her honour.

A surprise in store!

Entertainers travelled from joust to joust.

DANCING BEAR

WOW! That was so exciting! What a FANTASTIC day!

It sure was, Henry. I kept on being fed titbits by people in the crowd.

JUGGLER

PIE STALL

Minstrels wrote and sang songs. Some songs were old favourites, some told up-to-date news.

COME GATHER YE ROUND!

I like a good tune!

HOWWWL!

This instrument is called a lute.

Boar's head was a very popular (special) dish.

A gallery of castles

Banquet

Lords, ladies and knights sat at "top table" on a platform.

TOP TABLE

HORN OF WINE

The lower table was made of loose planks. It was taken down after meals.

People ate with their fingers.

BENCHES

CHAIRS

Wandering minstrels went from castle to castle. As well as singing, they told stories.

PLING!

ROAST SWAN

Scraps were thrown on the floor for the dogs.

TABLECLOTH

This is the life!

Trenchers

Most people ate off thick slices of stale bread (not plates). These were called trenchers. Some of the juices soaked into the trenchers. They were then given to the poor to eat.

TRENCHER

At the end of the day

Glossary

Archer: someone who shoots with a bow and arrow.

Cauldron: a great big round-bottomed cooking pot.

Chamber pot: a pot used by lords and ladies before proper flushing toilets were invented. It had to be emptied (by a servant, of course).

Chapel: a castle's private church.

Dovecote: a bird house where doves are kept (often for eating). Some dovecotes were built into the walls of buildings.

Dungeon: a castle's basement prison.

Embroidery: sewing patterns or pictures onto a cloth. A popular pastime with noble women.

Herald: a person who delivers messages and makes official announcements for important people.

Joust: a competition between knights on horses, using their lances to try to knock each other down.

Lance: a long wooden pole with a pointed metal end, used by knights when jousting to try to knock the other knight off his horse.

Mace: a heavy spiked club used as a weapon.

Morning star: a spiked metal ball attached to a wooden handle by a chain. Used by knights as a weapon.

Sceptre: a short, thick staff – often made of gold and studded with jewels – carried by a king to show his power.

Serfs: poor people – in other words most people – who owned very little and had to work for their lord and master (such as a baron). Most of them farmed the land. They had very few rights of their own.

Tournament: a big jousting competition.

Index

Henry's House

We hope you enjoyed your visit
to **Henry's House**
Come back soon!

Look out for:
- Bodies
- Creepy-crawlies
- Egyptians
- Dinosaurs
- Space

For more facts and fun, visit us at
www.headforhenryshouse.co.uk